# ARROW TO ALASKA

A Pacific Northwest Adventure

## HANNAH VIANO

little bigfoot

an imprint of sasquatch books
seattle, wa

Manufactured in China by C&C Offset Printing Co. Ltd.
Shenzhen, Guangdong Province, in February 2015

Published by Little Bigfoot,
an imprint of Sasquatch Books

20 19 18 17 16 15          9 8 7 6 5 4 3 2

Editor: Tegan Tigani
Project editor: Nancy W. Cortelyou
Design: Anna Goldstein
Illustrations: Hannah Viano
Library of Congress Cataloging-in-Publication
Data is available.

ISBN: 978-1-57061-949-6

Sasquatch Books
1904 Third Avenue, Suite 710
Seattle, WA 98101
(206) 467-4300
www.sasquatchbooks.com
custserv@sasquatchbooks.com

For S.K.Y. and J.F.V

Two known adventurers, who taught me to
dream up crazy ideas and then helped me go out
and live them.

Arrow was the usual small, grimy boy. He spent his afternoons swashbuckling the blackberry bushes and playing captain of the cedar stump in the backyard. At night he listened carefully for the "TOOoooooT! TOOT!" of boats calling for the bridge to open, sparking dreams brimming with adventure.

While crossing the Locks on his way to school in Seattle, Arrow wondered about the boats coming and going. Where was the cargo barge heading, and how many tropical islands had those barefoot sailors visited?

One day a letter came written with pencil on yellow lined paper. The writing was scraggly, and pictures filled the empty spaces. Fantastic fish jumped between words, and boats sailed off the page.

The letter was from Grampy Lightning in Alaska. He was coming to Seattle to visit. A note at the bottom read, "That grandson of mine needs to get out of the city. I could use a helper before I leave. Send him up."

For all of his six long years, Arrow watched boats go by and longed to be carried away by one of them. Within seconds of hearing Grampy's invitation, Arrow was racing around the house yelling *WAHOOooooos* and searching for his rubber boots.

Unfortunately, the next morning, Arrow's packing came to a screeching halt. His mother sat him down and said, "I'm sorry, Arrow, but it's not a good time for me to go with you to Grampy's."

"Maybe next year. . ."

At those words, the boy's heart fell. He sank into his bed and didn't even want a bedtime story.

That night he dreamed of a barge hauling his favorite ice cream. It had been lured onto the rocks by mermaids with bitter tongues.

A few days later, Arrow awoke to find Aunt Kelly (a known adventurer) drinking coffee at the kitchen table.

She had Grampy's letter in her hands. She also had a plan—a wonderful, perfect, excellent plan.

Aunt Kelly was captain of a salmon tender boat, the *Angie*, headed up the inside passage to Alaska. Arrow could go with her, as long as he kept out from underfoot.

Before long the big day
came, and Arrow was waving to
his mother from the deck of the *Angie*. The
huge metal doors of the Locks opened wide and
the unmistakable smell of saltwater rushed in.
They were off!

Past miles of islands and evergreen trees they steamed. Eagles looked on from tangled nests, and orca whales trailed silently in the *Angie*'s wake. The boy spent long hours watching the scene from a bench next to the helm with Huntley, the ship's cat, curled in his lap.

Night and day they traveled, with the crew working in shifts. The giant diesel stove always roared away in the galley, producing towering stacks of hotcakes, cast-iron skillets full of brownies, and endless pots of hot chocolate and coffee.

When they got close to the fishing grounds, humpback whales rose in greeting. The salmon fishermen in their small boats came alongside to sell the day's catch.

A sea of beautiful fish poured out of the sacks and onto the sorting tables. Arrow watched amazed as Kelly and her crew tossed fish this way and that. He almost wished he could stay on the *Angie* forever, but it was time to go meet someone.

Even from a distance he could see that Grampy Lightning's house was a magical thing.

Built onto a dozen giant old tree trunks strapped together, it floated on top of the water with decks and docks sticking out on all sides. Tomato plants and pole beans grew in an old clawfoot tub, and a dozen boats of all sizes were scattered around the place, some half built and others bobbing pleasantly along with the house.

"AHHOOOOOY there!" called a deep, dusty voice from the other end of the harbor. Arrow felt a hint of shyness coming on as the wrinkled old man rowed steadily towards them.

Grampy was not a pirate or the wild-eyed Captain Ahab the boy had imagined. He had a neatly trimmed mustache and wore a tidy wool vest with buttons.

In short time Arrow's shyness melted away. Grampy showed him around the floathouse, pointing out treasures from far off adventures and telling stories from a life spent messing about in boats.

They fished in the mornings and watched the stars from the deck at night. Come afternoons, the two worked together putting the finishing touches on Grampy Lightning's latest boat.

Soon leaving day came. Grampy bustled about the place tying and re-tying everything, readying the house to take care of itself for a while.

Arrow sat dangling his feet in the water and waiting to see who would come for them. "What sort of boat does your friend have, so I know what to look for?"

His grandfather just glanced up at the sky and said, "He'll be here soon enough, wait and see."

A few minutes later, there was the thunderous roar of an engine close overhead as a seaplane flew just above the little floathouse. It landed in front of them with a tremendous wave.

The boy still had his mouth open in surprise when a young man leaped out and gave his grandfather a warm hug. In moments they were all packed and roaring off out of the harbor.

Eyes glued to the window, Arrow watched as the floathouse disappeared behind them. The islands and coves where the *Angie* was working spread out below.

The plane turned south. With his grandfather's help the boy spotted places he remembered from the boat trip north.

The pilot retraced Arrow's route right up to the entrance to the Locks. They flew above the ship canal and down into the busy afternoon traffic on the waters of Lake Union.

From the next seat over, Grampy Lightning pointed ahead to a group of figures on the dock.

They waved excitedly, the same way Arrow had done many times, welcoming friends and family home. The not-quite-so-small boy looked back to see his grandfather break into a wide smile and ask, "So what's our next adventure?"

Arrow squinched his face, thinking hard. "Do they let children into Antarctica?"

# Cast-iron Skillet Brownies

*(Recipe by Jess Thomson)*

MAKES 10 TO 12 BIG BROWNIES

1 cup (2 sticks) unsalted butter, plus more for the pan, cut into small pieces

½ pound semisweet chocolate, finely chopped

3 large eggs

1 cup packed dark brown sugar

1 teaspoon vanilla extract

1 cup all-purpose flour

1 teaspoon baking powder

Pinch kosher salt

Preheat the oven to 350 degrees F. Butter a roughly 8-inch ovenproof skillet or square baking pan and set aside.

In a small saucepan, melt the butter and chocolate together over low heat, stirring frequently. Set aside.

In a mixing bowl, whisk together the eggs and brown sugar until thick. Whisk in the vanilla and the chocolate mixture, then add the flour, baking powder, and salt. Stir until well combined.

Pour the batter into the prepared pan and bake for 35 to 40 minutes, or until puffed and just beginning to crack in the center. Let the pan cool for 30 minutes on the counter.

Serve warm, sliced into wedges or squares, or let cool to room temperature, cover, and eat within a week or so, cutting just before serving.